- **Chapter 1: Understanding the Basics of SEO**
    - What is SEO? A comprehensive definition.
    - Key components of SEO: On-page, Off-page, and Technical SEO.
    - The role of search engines and how they work.
    - Common SEO myths and misconceptions.
- **Chapter 2: Keyword Research and Analysis**
    - The importance of keywords in SEO.
    - Tools and techniques for effective keyword research.
    - How to analyze keyword competition and search volume.
    - Creating a keyword strategy that aligns with your goals.
- **Chapter 3: On-Page SEO Optimization**
    - Best practices for optimizing individual web pages.
    - How to create SEO-friendly content (titles, meta descriptions, headers, etc.).
    - The importance of user experience (UX) in on-page SEO.
    - Optimizing images, videos, and other media for SEO.
- **Chapter 4: Technical SEO Fundamentals**
    - Understanding website structure and its impact on SEO.
    - How to improve site speed, mobile-friendliness, and security.
    - The role of XML sitemaps, robots.txt, and canonical tags.
    - Tools for monitoring and fixing technical SEO issues.
- **Chapter 5: Off-Page SEO and Link Building**
    - What is off-page SEO and why it matters?
    - Strategies for building high-quality backlinks.
    - The role of social media and influencer marketing in SEO.
    - How to avoid black hat SEO practices that can harm your site.

- **Chapter 6: Local SEO Strategies**
  - The importance of local SEO for businesses targeting specific geographic areas.
  - How to optimize for Google My Business and local search results.
  - Strategies for gathering and managing online reviews.
  - Tools and techniques for local keyword research.
- **Chapter 7: Content Marketing and SEO Integration**
  - The relationship between content marketing and SEO.
  - How to create content that attracts both search engines and readers.
  - The importance of content updates and repurposing for SEO.
  - Case studies of successful content-driven SEO strategies.
- **Chapter 8: SEO Tools and How to Use Them**
  - Overview of essential SEO tools (free and paid).
  - How to use Google Analytics and Google Search Console for SEO.
  - Tools for keyword research, site audits, and backlink analysis.
  - Tips for selecting the right tools based on your needs and budget.
- **Chapter 9: Measuring and Tracking SEO Success**
  - Key metrics to track for SEO success (traffic, rankings, conversions, etc.).
  - How to set up and use SEO dashboards.
  - The role of A/B testing and experimentation in SEO.
  - How to report SEO results to stakeholders.
- **Chapter 10: Staying Updated with SEO Trends**
  - The ever-changing nature of SEO and why staying updated is crucial.
  - How to keep up with algorithm updates and industry changes.
  - Resources for ongoing SEO education and learning.
  - Predictions for the future of SEO.

- **Introduction: The Importance of SEO in Today's Digital Landscape**
    - Search Engine Optimization (SEO) is more critical than ever today but so is Search EVERYWHERE Optimization. With millions of websites competing for attention, effective SEO practices can make the difference between being discovered by your target audience or getting lost in the vast expanse of the internet. SEO is the process of optimizing your online content so that search engines like Google can easily understand it and present it to users searching for relevant information.
    - The impact of SEO on a website's visibility, traffic, and success cannot be overstated. Businesses, bloggers, and content creators who understand and apply SEO principles are more likely to rank higher in search results, attract more visitors, and ultimately achieve their online goals.
    - Throughout this book, you'll learn how to conduct effective keyword research, optimize your web pages, enhance your site's technical performance, build high-quality backlinks, and measure your SEO success. Additionally, you'll explore the latest tools and trends that are shaping the future of SEO.

Table of Contents

Chapter 1: Understanding the Basics of SEO 6

Chapter 2: Keyword Research and Analysis 10

Chapter 3: On-Page SEO Optimization 15

Chapter 4: Technical SEO Fundamentals 19

Chapter 5: Off-Page SEO and Link Building 24

Chapter 6: Local SEO Strategies 29

Chapter 7: Content Marketing and SEO Integration 36

Chapter 8: SEO Tools and How to Use Them 42

Chapter 9: Measuring and Tracking SEO Success 48

Chapter 10: Staying Updated with SEO Trends 55

Conclusion and Final Thoughts 61

Appendix: Resources and Tools 62

- **Conclusion: Building a Sustainable SEO Strategy**
  - Recap of key takeaways from the book.
  - The importance of continuous learning and adaptation in SEO.
  - Final thoughts on the long-term benefits of a strong SEO strategy.
- **Appendix: Resources and Tools**
  - Recommended tools and platforms for SEO.
  - Further reading and learning resources.
  - Citations and references used throughout the book.

Chapter 1: Understanding the Basics of SEO

Search Engine Optimization (SEO) is a multifaceted discipline that involves optimizing various elements of a website to improve its visibility in search engine results pages (SERPs). The goal of SEO is to attract organic (non-paid) traffic to your site by ensuring that it ranks highly for relevant search queries. With over 3.5 billion Google searches conducted each day, according to Internet Live Stats (2024), mastering SEO is essential for any business or content creator looking to succeed online.

What is SEO? A Comprehensive Definition

SEO encompasses a range of strategies and techniques aimed at improving a website's visibility in search engines like Google, Bing, and Yahoo. These strategies can be broadly categorized into three main areas: on-page SEO, off-page SEO, and technical SEO. Each plays a crucial role in helping search engines understand your content and deliver it to users who are searching for information, products, or services.

- **On-Page SEO** focuses on optimizing the content and HTML source code of individual pages. This includes the use of keywords, meta descriptions, title tags, and headers, all of which help search engines understand the content of your page.

- **Off-Page SEO** involves actions taken outside of your website to impact its ranking. The most notable aspect of off-page SEO is link building, where other reputable sites link back to your content, signaling to search engines that your site is authoritative and valuable.

- **Technical SEO** refers to optimizing the backend structure of your website to ensure that search engines can crawl and index your site effectively. This includes site speed, mobile-friendliness, security, and proper use of sitemaps and robots.txt files.

Understanding these components is the first step in creating an effective SEO strategy that drives traffic and improves your site's ranking.

The Role of Search Engines and How They Work

To fully grasp the importance of SEO, it's essential to understand how search engines work. Search engines like Google use complex algorithms to crawl, index, and rank content across the web. These algorithms are designed to deliver the most relevant and authoritative results based on a user's search query.

- **Crawling:** Search engines use bots, known as spiders or crawlers, to scour the internet and find new content. These crawlers follow links from one page to another, discovering new URLs that can be indexed.

- **Indexing:** Once a page is crawled, it's stored in a massive database called an index. Here, the content is analyzed and categorized based on various factors, including keywords, meta tags, and overall content quality.

- **Ranking:** When a user enters a search query, the search engine retrieves relevant results from its index and ranks them based on a variety of factors, including relevance, authority, and user experience.

Google's algorithm, for instance, takes into account over 200 ranking factors, with some of the most important being backlinks, content quality, and mobile-friendliness. In 2023, Google introduced the Helpful Content Update, which prioritizes content that is created primarily for people rather than for the purpose of ranking in search engines. This update underscores the importance of creating high-quality, user-focused content as part of your SEO strategy.

Key Components of SEO: On-Page, Off-Page, and Technical SEO

Each component of SEO plays a vital role in improving your site's visibility and driving organic traffic. Here's a closer look at each:

- **On-Page SEO:** This involves optimizing the content and HTML elements on your website. Key practices include using relevant keywords, crafting compelling meta descriptions, and optimizing title tags and headers. In 2024, keyword optimization continues to be crucial, but search engines are increasingly focused on understanding the intent behind search queries. This means that your content should not only include keywords but also address the needs and questions of your audience.

- **Off-Page SEO:** Building a strong backlink profile remains one of the most important off-page SEO strategies. According to a study by Backlinko in 2023, the top-ranking pages on Google have an average of 3.8 times more backlinks than those that rank in positions 2-10. However, not all backlinks are created equal. Focus on earning links from reputable, high-authority websites within your industry.

- **Technical SEO:** Ensuring that your website is technically sound is critical for search engines to crawl and index your site efficiently. In 2024, site speed and mobile-friendliness are more important than ever, especially with the continued rollout of Google's Core Web Vitals as a ranking factor. A report by Google (2023) found that 53% of mobile users abandon sites that take longer than three seconds to load, highlighting the importance of optimizing site speed.

Common SEO Myths and Misconceptions

Despite the abundance of information available, there are still many myths and misconceptions surrounding SEO. Understanding the truth behind these myths is crucial for implementing an effective strategy.

- **Myth 1: SEO is a one-time effort.** Many believe that SEO is something you can set and forget, but in reality, it's an ongoing process. Search engine algorithms are constantly evolving, and so should your SEO strategy. Regularly updating content, monitoring keyword performance, and adapting to algorithm changes are essential for maintaining and improving your rankings.

- **Myth 2: More keywords mean better rankings.** While keywords are important, stuffing your content with them can actually harm your rankings. This practice, known as keyword stuffing, is penalized by search engines. Instead, focus on creating valuable content that naturally incorporates relevant keywords.

- **Myth 3: Backlinks from any site are beneficial.** Not all backlinks are equal. Links from low-quality or spammy sites can negatively impact your SEO. It's better to have fewer high-quality backlinks than a large number of low-quality ones. In 2024, search engines continue to prioritize the quality of backlinks over quantity.

Laying the Foundation for Effective SEO

Understanding the basics of SEO is the first step in building a successful online presence. By grasping the fundamental concepts of on-page, off-page, and technical SEO, as well as how search engines operate, you can begin to implement strategies that improve your site's visibility and attract more organic traffic. In the next chapter, we'll dive into keyword research and analysis, exploring how to identify the right keywords that will drive traffic and conversions.

Chapter 2: Keyword Research and Analysis

Keywords are the foundation of SEO but not where the buck stops. They are the words and phrases that users type into search engines when looking for information, products, or services. Identifying the right keywords for your content is crucial for attracting the right audience and improving your website's visibility in search engine results pages (SERPs). According to Ahrefs, 92.42% of keywords get ten monthly searches or fewer, highlighting the importance of targeting the right keywords to capture valuable search traffic. In this chapter, we'll explore the importance of keyword research, tools and techniques for effective keyword analysis, and how to create a keyword strategy that aligns with your goals.

The Importance of Keywords in SEO

Keywords serve as the bridge between what people are searching for and the content you are providing. When used effectively, they help search engines understand the relevance of your content to specific queries. This, in turn, increases your chances of ranking higher in SERPs, driving more organic traffic to your website.

However, it's not just about finding any keywords—it's about finding the right ones. The most effective keywords are those that are relevant to your content, have a decent search volume, and aren't overly competitive. Google's BERT update in 2019 shifted the focus even more toward understanding the context and intent behind search queries, making it essential to consider the user's search intent when selecting keywords.

Tools and Techniques for Effective Keyword Research

Keyword research is a critical step in any SEO strategy. It involves identifying the words and phrases that your target audience is using to find content related to your niche. Here are some tools and techniques to help you conduct effective keyword research:

1. Google Keyword Planner:
- **Overview:** Google Keyword Planner is a free tool that provides keyword ideas and search volume data based on real Google searches. It's an excellent starting point for discovering new keywords and understanding how often specific keywords are searched.

- **How to Use:** Enter a broad term related to your industry, and Google Keyword Planner will generate a list of related keywords, along with data on search volume, competition, and cost-per-click (CPC) for paid advertising. Focus on keywords with moderate search volume and low to medium competition.

2. Ahrefs Keywords Explorer:

- **Overview:** Ahrefs is a powerful SEO tool that offers in-depth keyword research capabilities. Its Keywords Explorer provides data on keyword difficulty, search volume, and click-through rates, among other metrics.
- **How to Use:** Enter a keyword into Ahrefs Keywords Explorer to get a comprehensive analysis, including the number of clicks that keyword receives, related keywords, and the top-ranking pages for that keyword. Use this data to refine your keyword strategy and identify less competitive keywords with high traffic potential.

3. SEMrush Keyword Magic Tool:

- **Overview:** SEMrush's Keyword Magic Tool is another popular choice for keyword research. It provides a vast database of keywords, along with insights into search volume, trends, and keyword difficulty.
- **How to Use:** Use the Keyword Magic Tool to generate keyword ideas based on a seed keyword. SEMrush allows you to filter keywords by broad match, phrase match, exact match, and related terms, making it easier to find long-tail keywords that align with your content.

4. Ubersuggest:

- **Overview:** Ubersuggest, created by Neil Patel, is a free keyword research tool that provides keyword suggestions, search volume, and SEO difficulty data. It also offers insights into content ideas and backlink opportunities.
- **How to Use:** Enter a keyword or domain into Ubersuggest to get a list of keyword ideas, along with metrics like search volume and competition. Ubersuggest also provides content suggestions based on popular articles related to your keywords.

5. Google Trends:

- **Overview:** Google Trends is a free tool that shows the popularity of a search term over time. It's useful for identifying seasonal trends and emerging topics in your industry.
- **How to Use:** Enter a keyword into Google Trends to see how its popularity has changed over time. You can also compare multiple keywords to determine which one is more popular. Use this data to capitalize on trending topics or avoid keywords that are declining in popularity.

How to Analyze Keyword Competition and Search Volume

Once you've generated a list of potential keywords, the next step is to analyze their competition and search volume. Understanding these factors will help you prioritize which keywords to target.

1. Search Volume:

- **What It Is:** Search volume refers to the number of times a keyword is searched within a specific period, usually monthly. High search volume indicates a popular keyword, but it also often means more competition.
- **How to Use It:** Look for keywords with moderate to high search volume, but balance this with competition. While high-volume keywords can drive significant traffic, they may be harder to rank for. Consider targeting long-tail keywords—phrases with three or more words—that have lower search volume but are easier to rank for and often more aligned with user intent.

2. Keyword Difficulty:

- **What It Is:** Keyword difficulty (KD) is a metric that estimates how hard it will be to rank for a specific keyword. Tools like Ahrefs and SEMrush provide KD scores, typically on a scale of 0-100, with higher scores indicating more competition.
- **How to Use It:** Focus on keywords with a KD score that matches your website's authority and resources. If your site is relatively new or has a low domain authority, target keywords with a lower KD score to improve your chances of ranking.

3. Search Intent:

- **What It Is:** Search intent refers to the purpose behind a user's search query. Understanding whether the intent is informational, navigational, transactional, or commercial is crucial for selecting the right keywords.
- **How to Use It:** Align your content with the search intent of your target keywords. For example, if the intent is informational, focus on providing in-depth content that answers questions. If the intent is transactional, optimize product pages or service descriptions to facilitate conversions.

Creating a Keyword Strategy That Aligns with Your Goals

A successful keyword strategy goes beyond simply identifying popular keywords. It involves aligning those keywords with your business goals, audience needs, and content strategy. Here's how to create a keyword strategy that drives results:

1. Define Your Goals:

- **What to Do:** Start by defining what you want to achieve with your SEO efforts. Whether it's increasing organic traffic, generating leads, or boosting sales, your goals will guide your keyword selection.
- **How to Apply:** Choose keywords that align with your goals. For example, if your goal is to increase sales, focus on transactional keywords that indicate purchase intent. If you want to build brand awareness, target informational keywords that draw users at the top of the funnel.

2. Organize Keywords by Topic Clusters:

- **What to Do:** Group related keywords into topic clusters, with a primary keyword as the main focus and related keywords as supporting topics. This approach helps you create content that covers a topic comprehensively, improving your chances of ranking for multiple related queries.
- **How to Apply:** Create pillar content that targets your primary keyword, and then develop supporting content that links back to the pillar page. This interlinking strategy enhances your site's structure and helps search engines understand the relationships between your content.

3. Monitor and Adjust Your Strategy:

- **What to Do:** SEO is an ongoing process, and your keyword strategy should be flexible. Regularly monitor your keyword performance, track rankings, and adjust your strategy based on what's working and what's not.

- **How to Apply:** Use tools like Google Search Console and Ahrefs to track keyword rankings and organic traffic. If certain keywords are underperforming, consider updating your content or shifting your focus to other keywords that show more potential.

The Foundation of Effective SEO

Keyword research and analysis are at the core of any successful SEO strategy. By identifying the right keywords and understanding their competition, search volume, and intent, you can create content that resonates with your audience and ranks well in search engines. In the next chapter, we'll explore on-page SEO optimization, focusing on how to optimize individual web pages for better rankings and user experience.

Chapter 3: On-Page SEO Optimization

On-page SEO is the practice of optimizing individual web pages to rank higher in search engines and attract more relevant traffic. It involves various elements, from the content itself to the HTML source code, and plays a crucial role in ensuring that your website is both search engine-friendly and user-friendly. According to a 2023 report by Backlinko, pages that rank in the top 10 positions on Google have an average on-page optimization score of 92%. This chapter will cover the best practices for on-page SEO, including how to create SEO-friendly content, the importance of user experience, and optimizing media like images and videos.

Best Practices for On-Page SEO Optimization

On-page SEO encompasses a wide range of factors that influence how search engines understand and rank your content. Here's how to optimize these elements effectively:

1. Crafting SEO-Friendly Content:

- **Title Tags:** The title tag is one of the most important on-page SEO elements. It should be concise (50-60 characters), include your primary keyword, and clearly convey the topic of the page. According to Moz, title tags that start with a keyword have been shown to perform better than those with the keyword towards the end.

- **Meta Descriptions:** While meta descriptions don't directly affect rankings, they influence click-through rates (CTR). A compelling meta description (up to 155 characters) that includes your primary keyword can entice users to click on your result in the SERPs. A 2024 study by SEMrush found that optimized meta descriptions could improve CTR by up to 30%.

- **Headers (H1, H2, H3):** Headers help structure your content and make it easier for both users and search engines to navigate. The H1 tag should include your primary keyword and clearly represent the main topic of the page. Use H2 and H3 tags to break up the content into sections, making it more readable and scannable.

2. Optimizing Content for Keywords:

- **Keyword Placement:** Place your primary keyword in the title tag, meta description, URL, and the first 100 words of your content. However, avoid keyword stuffing—a practice that can lead to penalties. Instead, aim for a natural keyword density of around 1-2%, incorporating related terms and synonyms.

- **Content Length:** There's no one-size-fits-all answer for content length, but longer, more in-depth content tends to perform better in search rankings. A 2023 analysis by HubSpot revealed that the average word count of top-ranking pages is between 1,500 and 2,000 words. Focus on providing comprehensive, valuable content that thoroughly covers the topic.

- **Internal Linking:** Internal links connect your pages and help search engines understand the structure of your website. They also keep users on your site longer by guiding them to related content. Aim to include 2-3 internal links per page, using descriptive anchor text that includes relevant keywords.

3. The Importance of User Experience (UX) in On-Page SEO:

- **Mobile-Friendliness:** With over 60% of searches now conducted on mobile devices (Google, 2023), having a mobile-friendly website is essential. Ensure that your site is responsive, meaning it adapts to different screen sizes and devices. Google's Mobile-Friendly Test tool can help you assess your site's performance.

- **Site Speed:** Page speed is a confirmed ranking factor, and slow-loading pages can lead to high bounce rates. Google's Core Web Vitals update, which became a ranking signal in 2021, emphasizes the importance of loading speed, interactivity, and visual stability. Aim for a page load time of under 2 seconds, as studies show that 53% of mobile users abandon sites that take longer than that to load (Google, 2023).

- **Readability:** Your content should be easy to read and understand. Use short paragraphs, bullet points, and subheadings to break up the text. Tools like Hemingway App can help you simplify your writing and improve readability. Aim for a readability score of 8th grade or lower to ensure your content is accessible to a broad audience.

4. Optimizing Images, Videos, and Other Media for SEO:

- **Image Optimization:** Images play a crucial role in on-page SEO, but they can also slow down your site if not properly optimized. Compress images to reduce file size without compromising quality, and use descriptive file names and alt text that include relevant keywords. Alt text not only helps with SEO but also improves accessibility for users with visual impairments.

- **Video SEO:** Videos are increasingly important in SEO, as they can increase user engagement and time spent on your site. To optimize videos, use a video sitemap, host videos on a platform like YouTube or Vimeo, and include transcripts and captions. A 2023 study by Wyzowl found that including a video on a landing page can increase conversions by up to 80%.

- **Rich Media (Infographics, Interactive Elements):** Rich media like infographics and interactive content can enhance user engagement and shareability. Optimize these elements by ensuring they load quickly and are responsive across devices. Additionally, use schema markup to help search engines understand and index this content.

Optimizing URLs and Site Structure

Your site's structure and URLs are also important aspects of on-page SEO. A well-organized site structure makes it easier for search engines to crawl and index your content, while SEO-friendly URLs can improve click-through rates.

1. Creating SEO-Friendly URLs:

- **Simplicity:** Keep URLs short, descriptive, and easy to read. Avoid using special characters, and limit the use of numbers and unnecessary words. According to Backlinko, shorter URLs tend to rank higher in Google search results.

- **Keyword Inclusion:** Include your primary keyword in the URL to signal to search engines what the page is about. However, avoid keyword stuffing—focus on making the URL clear and descriptive.

- **Consistency:** Use a consistent URL structure throughout your site, with clear categories and subcategories if applicable. This not only helps with SEO but also improves user experience by making it easier for visitors to navigate your site.

2. Structuring Your Site for SEO:

- **Hierarchy:** Organize your site's content into a logical hierarchy, with main categories and subcategories. This structure helps search engines understand the relationships between pages and prioritize more important content.

- **Internal Linking:** As mentioned earlier, internal linking is key to creating a well-structured site. Link from category pages to individual articles, and from articles back to relevant category pages. This not only improves SEO but also enhances user navigation.
- **Breadcrumbs:** Breadcrumbs are navigational aids that show users their location within your site's hierarchy. They improve usability and can also enhance SEO by helping search engines understand the structure of your site.

Building a Strong On-Page SEO Foundation

On-page SEO is essential for ensuring that your website is optimized for both search engines and users. By following best practices for content creation, keyword placement, user experience, and media optimization, you can improve your site's rankings, drive more organic traffic, and provide a better experience for your visitors. In the next chapter, we'll dive into technical SEO fundamentals, focusing on the behind-the-scenes elements that are critical for your site's performance and visibility.

Chapter 4: Technical SEO Fundamentals

Technical SEO is the backbone of a well-optimized website. It involves optimizing the infrastructure of your site to ensure that search engines can crawl, index, and rank your content effectively. Without a solid technical foundation, even the best content and on-page SEO efforts can fall short. According to a 2024 survey by Search Engine Journal, 63% of SEO professionals consider technical SEO to be a top priority for improving website performance. In this chapter, we'll explore the key aspects of technical SEO, including website structure, site speed, mobile-friendliness, and tools for monitoring and fixing technical issues.

Understanding Website Structure and Its Impact on SEO

Website structure refers to how the pages on your site are organized and linked together. A well-structured site makes it easier for search engines to crawl and index your content, which can improve your rankings and visibility. Additionally, a clear and logical structure enhances user experience by making it easier for visitors to navigate your site.

1. Importance of a Logical Site Structure:

- **Crawlability:** Search engines use bots, or crawlers, to discover and index content on your website. A logical site structure ensures that all important pages are easily accessible to these crawlers. If your site is poorly structured, search engines may struggle to find and index your content, leading to lower rankings.

- **User Experience (UX):** A clear site structure improves UX by helping users find the information they're looking for quickly. A good structure reduces bounce rates and increases the time visitors spend on your site, both of which are positive signals to search engines.

- **Hierarchy:** Organize your site's content into a hierarchical structure, with main categories at the top and subcategories and individual pages beneath them. This hierarchy should be reflected in your site's navigation menu and internal linking strategy.

2. Creating an XML Sitemap:

- **What It Is:** An XML sitemap is a file that lists all the important pages on your website, helping search engines understand the structure of your site and find new content more efficiently. It's particularly useful for large sites or sites with complex structures.

- **How to Create It:** Most content management systems (CMS) like WordPress can automatically generate an XML sitemap. You can also use tools like Yoast SEO, Screaming Frog, or Google Search Console to create and submit your sitemap. Ensure that your sitemap is up to date and includes all critical pages.

3. **Utilizing Robots.txt:**

- **What It Is:** Robots.txt is a file that gives instructions to search engine crawlers about which pages or sections of your site they should or shouldn't crawl. This can be useful for preventing the indexing of duplicate content, admin pages, or other non-essential pages.

- **How to Use It:** Create a robots.txt file in the root directory of your website. Use this file to block crawlers from accessing pages that don't need to be indexed. However, be cautious when using robots.txt, as blocking important pages by mistake can hurt your SEO.

Improving Site Speed and Performance

Site speed is a critical factor in both user experience and SEO. Slow-loading sites can frustrate users and lead to higher bounce rates, which can negatively impact your rankings. Google's Core Web Vitals update, which rolled out in 2021, emphasizes the importance of site speed, interactivity, and visual stability as ranking factors.

1. **Analyzing and Optimizing Site Speed:**

- **Core Web Vitals:** Core Web Vitals are a set of metrics that Google uses to assess a site's loading performance, interactivity, and visual stability. These include Largest Contentful Paint (LCP), First Input Delay (FID), and Cumulative Layout Shift (CLS).

- **Tools for Testing Site Speed:** Use tools like Google PageSpeed Insights, GTmetrix, or Lighthouse to analyze your site's speed and performance. These tools provide detailed reports on how your site performs in terms of Core Web Vitals and offer recommendations for improvement.

- **Optimization Techniques:** Compress images, minify CSS and JavaScript files, leverage browser caching, and use a content delivery network (CDN) to reduce load times. According to a 2024 study by Google, websites that implement these optimizations see a 27% improvement in site speed on average.

2. **Mobile-Friendliness and Responsive Design:**

    - **The Mobile-First Index:** Google now predominantly uses the mobile version of a website for indexing and ranking. This shift underscores the importance of having a mobile-friendly website that delivers a seamless experience across devices.

    - **Responsive Design:** Ensure that your site uses responsive design, meaning it automatically adjusts to fit the screen size of the device being used. A responsive site provides a better user experience and is more likely to rank well in mobile search results.

    - **Testing Mobile-Friendliness:** Use Google's Mobile-Friendly Test tool to check how well your site performs on mobile devices. The tool provides suggestions for improving mobile usability, such as increasing font size, optimizing buttons, and reducing page load times.

Security and HTTPS

Website security is another important aspect of technical SEO. Google considers site security when ranking websites, and sites that use HTTPS (Hypertext Transfer Protocol Secure) are more likely to rank higher than those that don't.

1. The Importance of HTTPS:

- **What It Is:** HTTPS is an internet communication protocol that protects the integrity and confidentiality of data between the user's computer and the site. It ensures that data exchanged between the user and the website is encrypted and secure.

- **Why It Matters:** In 2018, Google made HTTPS a ranking signal, and websites that don't use HTTPS are marked as "Not Secure" in the Chrome browser. This can negatively impact user trust and lead to lower rankings. As of 2024, over 95% of page one results on Google are HTTPS sites, according to Moz.

2. Implementing SSL Certificates:

- **What It Is:** An SSL (Secure Sockets Layer) certificate is a digital certificate that authenticates a website's identity and enables an encrypted connection. Installing an SSL certificate on your server activates HTTPS and allows secure connections from a web server to a browser.

- **How to Implement:** Purchase an SSL certificate from a reputable provider (many hosting companies offer them), and install it on your website. Some hosting providers also offer free SSL certificates through services like Let's Encrypt. After installation, ensure that all pages on your site redirect to the HTTPS version.

Tools for Monitoring and Fixing Technical SEO Issues

To maintain a healthy website and prevent technical issues from impacting your SEO, it's important to regularly monitor your site and address any problems that arise.

1. Google Search Console:

- **Overview:** Google Search Console is a free tool that helps you monitor your site's presence in Google search results. It provides insights into indexing issues, crawl errors, and security problems.
- **How to Use:** Regularly check Google Search Console for any issues that might affect your site's performance. Use the "Coverage" report to identify pages that aren't being indexed, and the "Mobile Usability" report to spot mobile-specific issues. Additionally, the "Core Web Vitals" report provides insights into your site's loading performance and user experience.

2. Screaming Frog SEO Spider:

- **Overview:** Screaming Frog is a powerful tool for auditing your website's technical SEO. It crawls your site and provides detailed reports on issues like broken links, duplicate content, missing meta tags, and more.
- **How to Use:** Run regular crawls of your site using Screaming Frog to identify and fix technical issues. The tool's reports can help you pinpoint areas that need optimization, such as slow-loading pages, thin content, or incorrect use of canonical tags.

3. Ahrefs Site Audit:

- **Overview:** Ahrefs offers a robust site audit tool that helps you identify and fix technical SEO issues. It provides detailed reports on factors like crawlability, performance, HTML tags, and social tags.
- **How to Use:** Use Ahrefs Site Audit to conduct regular technical SEO checks. The tool's "Health Score" gives you an overall rating of your

site's technical health, while detailed reports allow you to drill down into specific issues and address them promptly.

Strengthening Your Site's Technical SEO

Technical SEO is essential for ensuring that your website is well-structured, fast, secure, and mobile-friendly. By focusing on key areas like site structure, speed, mobile usability, and security, you can create a strong foundation that supports your content and on-page SEO efforts. In the next chapter, we'll explore off-page SEO and link building, focusing on strategies to boost your site's authority and improve its rankings.

Chapter 5: Off-Page SEO and Link Building

Off-page SEO refers to the actions taken outside of your own website to impact your rankings within search engine results pages (SERPs). While on-page SEO focuses on optimizing elements within your control, off-page SEO is primarily about building your site's authority and trustworthiness through external factors, the most significant of which is link building. According to a 2023 report by Moz, backlinks are among the top three ranking factors in Google's algorithm. In this chapter, we'll explore the importance of off-page SEO, effective link-building strategies, and how to avoid harmful practices that could negatively impact your site's performance.

What is Off-Page SEO and Why It Matters?

Off-page SEO encompasses all the activities you do outside your website to improve your rankings. The most important off-page SEO factor is backlinks, which are links from other websites to your own. Search engines view backlinks as votes of confidence in your content; the more high-quality links you have, the more authoritative and trustworthy your site appears.

1. The Role of Backlinks in SEO:

- **Authority and Trust:** Backlinks from reputable websites signal to search engines that your content is valuable and credible. This can significantly boost your site's authority, helping it rank higher for relevant keywords. A 2023 study by Ahrefs found that 90.63% of pages with no backlinks receive no organic traffic from Google, underscoring the importance of building a strong backlink profile.

- **Referral Traffic:** In addition to improving your rankings, backlinks can drive referral traffic from other websites. If a popular blog or news site links to your content, users who click on the link can become valuable visitors to your site.

- **Indexing:** Backlinks also help search engines discover your content. When search engine crawlers follow links from other websites to yours, they can more easily find and index new pages on your site.

2. The Importance of Building High-Quality Backlinks:

- **Relevance:** Not all backlinks are created equal. Links from websites that are relevant to your industry or niche carry more weight than links from unrelated sites. For example, if you run a fitness blog, a backlink from a health and wellness site is more valuable than one from a general news site.

- **Authority:** The authority of the linking site also matters. A backlink from a high-authority site like The New York Times or Forbes will have a more significant impact on your rankings than a link from a lesser-known or lower-quality site. Tools like Moz's Domain Authority (DA) or Ahrefs' Domain Rating (DR) can help you assess the authority of potential linking sites.

- **Dofollow vs. Nofollow:** Dofollow links pass SEO value (or "link juice") to your site, while nofollow links do not. While dofollow links are more beneficial for SEO, nofollow links can still drive valuable referral traffic and build brand awareness.

Effective Link-Building Strategies

Building high-quality backlinks requires a strategic approach. Here are some proven link-building strategies to help you increase your site's authority and improve your rankings:

1. Guest Blogging:

- **Overview:** Guest blogging involves writing articles for other websites in your industry in exchange for a backlink to your site. It's a mutually beneficial strategy: the host site gets quality content, and you get a backlink and exposure to a new audience.

- **How to Implement:** Identify reputable websites in your niche that accept guest posts. Reach out to them with a pitch that outlines your proposed topic and why it would be valuable to their audience. Ensure that your guest post is well-researched, relevant, and includes a natural link back to your site.

2. Content Marketing and Linkable Assets:

- **Overview:** Creating high-quality, shareable content (known as linkable assets) is one of the most effective ways to earn backlinks. Linkable assets can include in-depth blog posts, infographics, research reports, or tools and calculators.

- **How to Implement:** Focus on creating content that provides significant value to your audience and stands out in your industry. Promote your content through outreach to influencers, bloggers, and journalists who may find it useful and link to it. For example, a well-researched industry report with original data is more likely to attract backlinks than a generic blog post.

3. Broken Link Building:

- **Overview:** Broken link building involves finding broken links on other websites and suggesting your content as a replacement. This strategy helps site owners fix issues on their pages while earning you a valuable backlink.

- **How to Implement:** Use tools like Ahrefs' Broken Link Checker or Screaming Frog to find broken links on relevant websites. Reach out to the site owner or webmaster, informing them of the broken link and suggesting your content as a replacement. Be sure to explain why your content is a good fit and how it adds value.

4. Skyscraper Technique:

- **Overview:** The Skyscraper Technique involves finding popular content in your niche, creating something even better, and reaching out to the right people to earn backlinks. This strategy works because it capitalizes on proven interest while offering something new or improved.

- **How to Implement:** Start by identifying top-performing content in your industry using tools like BuzzSumo or Ahrefs Content Explorer. Analyze the content to see where you can improve—whether it's updating outdated information, adding more detail, or presenting it in a more visually appealing format. Once your content is published, reach out to sites that linked to the original content, informing them of your improved version and suggesting they link to it.

5. Influencer Outreach:

- **Overview:** Partnering with influencers in your industry can help you earn backlinks and gain exposure to a broader audience. Influencers can include bloggers, social media personalities, or industry experts who have a large following and the ability to drive traffic.

- **How to Implement:** Identify influencers who are relevant to your niche and have an engaged audience. Reach out to them with a proposal for collaboration, such as a sponsored post, product review, or interview. Ensure that the partnership is mutually beneficial and aligns with both parties' goals.

Avoiding Black Hat SEO Practices

While building backlinks is essential for SEO, it's important to avoid black hat SEO practices—unethical techniques that violate search engine guidelines and can result in penalties. Google's Penguin update, introduced in 2012, targets websites that engage in manipulative link-building tactics.

1. Understanding Black Hat SEO:

- **What It Is:** Black hat SEO refers to practices that are designed to manipulate search engine rankings through deceptive or unethical means. These practices include buying backlinks, participating in link farms, using automated link-building tools, and creating spammy or low-quality content purely for the sake of link building.

- **Why It's Harmful:** Engaging in black hat SEO can lead to severe penalties, including being de-indexed from search engines. Even if these tactics yield short-term gains, the long-term consequences can be devastating to your site's visibility and reputation.

2. Focus on Quality Over Quantity:

- **What to Do:** Instead of trying to build as many backlinks as possible, focus on earning high-quality, relevant links from reputable websites. A few links from authoritative sites are far more valuable than hundreds of low-quality links.

- **How to Apply:** Prioritize building relationships with industry peers, creating valuable content, and following ethical link-building practices. Always aim to add value to the internet rather than simply trying to game the system.

Building a Strong Off-Page SEO Strategy

Off-page SEO, particularly link building, is crucial for boosting your site's authority and improving your search engine rankings. By focusing on high-quality backlinks, ethical practices, and proven strategies like guest blogging and content marketing, you can build a strong off-page SEO foundation that supports your overall SEO efforts. In the next chapter, we'll explore local SEO strategies, focusing on how to optimize your site for local search results and attract customers in your geographic area.

Chapter 6: Local SEO Strategies

Local SEO is essential for businesses that serve specific geographic areas, as it helps you reach potential customers in your vicinity. Whether you run a brick-and-mortar store, offer services in a particular city, or operate within a defined region, optimizing your site for local search can significantly impact your visibility and success. According to Google, nearly 46% of all searches have a local intent, and 76% of people who search for something nearby visit a business within a day. In this chapter, we'll explore the importance of local SEO, how to optimize for Google My Business, strategies for gathering and managing online reviews, and tools for local keyword research.

The Importance of Local SEO for Businesses

Local SEO focuses on optimizing your online presence to attract more business from relevant local searches. These searches typically include location-specific keywords or search queries with local intent, such as "plumber near me" or "best coffee shop in [city]." Optimizing for local search helps you stand out in local search results, particularly in Google's Local Pack, which features the top three local business listings.

1. Enhancing Visibility in Local Searches:

- **Local Pack:** The Local Pack appears at the top of Google's search results for queries with local intent, displaying three local businesses along with their location on Google Maps. Appearing in the Local Pack can significantly increase your business's visibility, as it's often the first thing users see when searching for local services or products.

- **Organic Local Results:** In addition to the Local Pack, local SEO can improve your rankings in organic search results for location-specific queries. This is particularly important for businesses that rely on local customers, as it drives more targeted traffic to your website.

2. Driving Foot Traffic and Conversions:

- **Foot Traffic:** Local SEO is not just about online visibility—it directly impacts foot traffic to your physical location. A 2023 study by BrightLocal found that 78% of local mobile searches result in an offline purchase, underscoring the importance of local SEO for driving in-store visits.

- **Conversions:** By optimizing your site for local search, you can attract more qualified leads who are likely to convert into customers. This is particularly true for service-based businesses, where local SEO helps connect you with people actively searching for the services you offer.

Optimizing for Google My Business

Google My Business (GMB) is a free tool that allows businesses to manage their online presence across Google, including Search and Maps. Optimizing your GMB profile is one of the most effective ways to improve your local SEO and attract more customers.

1. Claiming and Verifying Your GMB Profile:

- **What It Is:** Claiming your GMB profile is the first step in taking control of your business's online presence. Verification confirms that you are the rightful owner or manager of the business, allowing you to manage the information that appears in Google Search and Maps.

- **How to Do It:** To claim your GMB profile, search for your business on Google and select "Claim this business" if it appears. If your business is not listed, you can create a new profile from scratch. Once claimed, Google will send you a verification code by mail, phone, or email, which you'll need to enter to complete the process.

2. Optimizing Your GMB Profile:

- **Business Information:** Ensure that all information on your GMB profile is accurate, up-to-date, and consistent with the details on your website and other online directories. This includes your business name, address, phone number (NAP), website URL, and hours of operation. Consistency across platforms is key to building trust with both search engines and potential customers.

- **Business Categories:** Choose the most relevant primary category for your business, and add secondary categories if applicable. Categories help Google understand what your business offers and match you with relevant local searches.

- **Business Description:** Write a clear and concise business description that includes relevant keywords. This description should highlight what makes your business unique and why customers should choose you over competitors.

- **Photos and Videos:** High-quality photos and videos can make your GMB profile more appealing and engaging. Include images of your storefront, products, services, and team members. According to Google, businesses with photos receive 42% more requests for directions and 35% more click-throughs to their websites.

3. Utilizing GMB Features:

- **Posts:** GMB allows you to create posts to share updates, promotions, events, and news directly on your profile. Regularly posting can keep your audience engaged and informed about what's happening at your business.

- **Q&A:** The Q&A section lets customers ask questions about your business, which you can respond to directly. Monitoring and answering these questions not only helps potential customers but also shows that you're attentive and responsive.

- **Bookings:** If your business offers appointments or reservations, you can enable the booking feature on GMB. This allows customers to book services directly from your GMB profile, making it more convenient for them to choose your business.

Strategies for Gathering and Managing Online Reviews

Online reviews are a crucial component of local SEO. Positive reviews not only boost your reputation but also influence your rankings in local search results. According to BrightLocal's 2023 Local Consumer Review Survey, 87% of consumers read online reviews for local businesses, with 79% trusting them as much as personal recommendations.

1. Encouraging Customer Reviews:

- **Ask for Reviews:** The simplest way to get more reviews is to ask your customers directly. Whether in person, through email, or via text, let your satisfied customers know how much you appreciate their feedback and encourage them to leave a review.

- **Make It Easy:** Provide clear instructions on how customers can leave a review, and include links to your GMB profile or other review platforms in your communications. The easier you make it for customers to leave a review, the more likely they are to do so.

- **Incentivize Reviews:** While it's important to avoid unethical practices like paying for reviews, you can incentivize reviews by offering discounts, freebies, or entry into a contest. Just be sure to follow Google's guidelines to avoid penalties.

2. Responding to Reviews:

- **Engage with Customers:** Responding to reviews, both positive and negative, shows that you value customer feedback and are committed to providing excellent service. A thoughtful response to a positive review can reinforce customer loyalty, while a well-handled response to a negative review can mitigate potential damage.

- **Be Professional:** Always maintain a professional tone when responding to reviews, even if the feedback is critical. Thank customers for their feedback, address any concerns, and offer solutions if necessary. This demonstrates that you take customer satisfaction seriously.

3. Managing Negative Reviews:

- **Addressing Issues:** When dealing with negative reviews, it's important to address the issue directly and offer a resolution. Apologize if necessary, and explain how you plan to prevent the issue from happening again. This can turn a negative experience into a positive one and show potential customers that you're proactive in addressing concerns.

- **Monitoring Reviews:** Regularly monitor your reviews across all platforms, including Google, Yelp, and social media. Tools like ReviewTrackers or Google Alerts can help you stay on top of new reviews and respond promptly.

Local Keyword Research and Optimization

Local keyword research involves identifying the search terms that potential customers in your area are using to find businesses like yours. Optimizing your site for these keywords can improve your visibility in local search results and drive more targeted traffic.

1. Conducting Local Keyword Research:

- **Use Local Modifiers:** Start by identifying primary keywords related to your business, then add local modifiers such as your city, neighborhood, or region. For example, instead of targeting "plumber," you might target "plumber in Austin" or "emergency plumber near me."

- **Google Keyword Planner:** Use Google Keyword Planner to find local keyword ideas and analyze search volume. This tool can help you identify popular search terms in your area and understand how competitive they are.

- **Google Trends:** Google Trends allows you to compare the popularity of different search terms over time and across geographic regions. Use this tool to identify emerging trends in your area and adjust your keyword strategy accordingly.

2. Optimizing Content for Local Keywords:

- **On-Page Optimization:** Incorporate local keywords into key on-page elements such as title tags, meta descriptions, headers, and content. Ensure that your NAP (name, address, phone number) is consistent across your website and other online listings.
- **Location Pages:** If your business serves multiple locations, create separate location pages for each area. These pages should include unique content tailored to the specific location, along with relevant local keywords.
- **Blog Content:** Consider creating blog posts or articles that focus on local events, news, or topics of interest. This not only helps with local SEO but also positions your business as an active and engaged member of the community.

Tools and Techniques for Local SEO Success

To maximize the effectiveness of your local SEO efforts, it's important to use the right tools and techniques. Here are some essential tools for local SEO:

1. Moz Local:

- **Overview:** Moz Local helps you manage your business listings across multiple directories, ensuring that your information is consistent and accurate. It also provides insights into your local SEO performance and helps you identify opportunities for improvement.
- **How to Use:** Use Moz Local to audit your current listings, update your NAP information, and monitor your presence on major local search platforms. The tool also tracks reviews and provides recommendations for optimizing your local SEO strategy.

2. BrightLocal:

- **Overview:** BrightLocal is an all-in-one local SEO platform that offers tools for local rank tracking, citation building, and review management. It's designed to help businesses improve their local search visibility and manage their online reputation.

- **How to Use:** Use BrightLocal's Rank Checker to track your rankings for local keywords, and the Citation Tracker to monitor your citations across the web. The Review Monitoring tool helps you stay on top of new reviews and respond promptly.

3. Google Search Console:

- **Overview:** Google Search Console is a free tool that provides valuable insights into how your site is performing in Google Search. It helps you monitor indexing issues, track keyword rankings, and understand how users are finding your site.
- **How to Use:** Use Google Search Console to identify keywords that are driving traffic to your site, including local search terms. The "Performance" report shows which queries are leading to clicks, impressions, and conversions, allowing you to refine your local SEO strategy.

Building a Strong Local SEO Presence

Local SEO is crucial for businesses that rely on local customers. By optimizing your Google My Business profile, gathering and managing online reviews, and conducting local keyword research, you can improve your visibility in local search results and attract more targeted traffic. In the next chapter, we'll explore how to integrate content marketing with SEO to create content that not only ranks well but also resonates with your audience.

Chapter 7: Content Marketing and SEO Integration

Content marketing and SEO are two sides of the same coin, and when integrated effectively, they can significantly enhance your online presence. While SEO focuses on optimizing your website and content for search engines, content marketing is about creating and distributing valuable content to attract and engage your audience. According to a 2023 report by HubSpot, businesses that prioritize blogging are 13 times more likely to see a positive return on investment (ROI). In this chapter, we'll explore how to align content marketing with SEO, strategies for creating content that ranks and resonates, and the importance of content updates and repurposing for long-term success.

The Relationship Between Content Marketing and SEO

Content marketing and SEO are closely intertwined. SEO helps ensure that your content is discoverable by search engines, while content marketing focuses on providing value to your audience. Together, they create a powerful strategy for driving organic traffic, building authority, and converting visitors into customers.

1. Content as the Foundation of SEO:

- **Keywords and Content:** Keywords are the bridge between your audience's search queries and your content. By conducting thorough keyword research (as discussed in Chapter 2) and incorporating those keywords into high-quality content, you can improve your chances of ranking for relevant searches. According to Backlinko, content that ranks on the first page of Google tends to be 1,890 words long, indicating that comprehensive content performs better in search engines.

- **Content Depth and Authority:** Search engines favor content that provides depth and authoritative insights on a topic. Creating in-depth content that thoroughly addresses a subject not only improves your SEO but also positions your brand as a thought leader in your industry. In 2023, Google's Helpful Content Update reinforced the importance of content that is created for users, not just for search engines.

2. Aligning Content with User Intent:

- **Understanding Search Intent:** Search intent refers to the reason behind a user's search query—whether they are looking for information, seeking to make a purchase, or comparing products. Aligning your content with the search intent of your target keywords is crucial for both SEO and content marketing success.

- **Types of Content for Different Intents:** Depending on the search intent, different types of content may be more appropriate. For example, blog posts and how-to guides are ideal for informational intent, while product pages and reviews are better suited for transactional intent. Creating content that matches the user's intent increases the likelihood of engagement and conversion.

3. Creating a Content Strategy That Supports SEO:

- **Topic Clusters and Pillar Pages:** A topic cluster strategy involves creating a pillar page that covers a broad topic in-depth, with supporting content (cluster content) that delves into related subtopics. This structure not only helps with SEO but also improves the user experience by providing a comprehensive resource on a particular subject.

- **Content Calendar:** Developing a content calendar helps ensure that your content marketing efforts are consistent and aligned with your SEO goals. Plan your content around high-priority keywords, seasonal trends, and industry events to maximize relevance and impact.

- **Evergreen Content:** Evergreen content is content that remains relevant and valuable over time, driving continuous traffic to your site. Examples include how-to guides, case studies, and resource lists. Focus on creating evergreen content that can be updated and repurposed to maintain its SEO value.

Strategies for Creating Content That Ranks and Resonates

Creating content that ranks well in search engines and resonates with your audience requires a combination of SEO best practices and content marketing principles. Here's how to achieve both:

1. Optimize Content for SEO:

- **On-Page SEO:** Ensure that your content is optimized for on-page SEO elements such as title tags, meta descriptions, headers, and internal links (as discussed in Chapter 3). Include your primary keyword in the title, first paragraph, and subheadings, but avoid keyword stuffing.

- **Readability and Engagement:** Content that is easy to read and engaging is more likely to rank well and keep visitors on your site. Use short paragraphs, bullet points, and visuals to break up the text and enhance readability. According to a 2023 study by SEMrush, content with images receives 94% more views than content without images.

- **Multimedia Integration:** Incorporating multimedia elements like videos, infographics, and interactive content can increase user engagement and time spent on your site. These metrics are positive signals to search engines and can improve your rankings.

2. Focus on Quality and Value:

- **Audience-Centric Content:** Create content that addresses the needs, pain points, and interests of your audience. Use tools like AnswerThePublic, Google Search Console, and social media listening to identify common questions and topics that resonate with your audience.

- **Original Research and Data:** Content that includes original research, data, and insights is more likely to attract backlinks and social shares, both of which are important for SEO. Consider conducting surveys, case studies, or experiments to generate unique data that adds value to your content.

- **Storytelling:** Storytelling is a powerful tool in content marketing, as it helps you connect with your audience on an emotional level. By weaving stories into your content, you can make it more relatable and memorable, which can increase engagement and shares.

3. Leveraging Long-Form Content:

- **Comprehensive Guides:** Long-form content, such as comprehensive guides and detailed tutorials, tends to perform well in search engines because it covers a topic thoroughly. HubSpot's 2023 research shows that blog posts with over 2,000 words receive more backlinks and social shares than shorter posts.

- **Content Skyscraping:** The Skyscraper Technique (mentioned in Chapter 5) involves finding top-performing content in your industry and creating a more comprehensive, updated, or visually appealing version. This strategy not only improves your chances of ranking but also attracts more links and shares.

- **User Experience (UX):** While long-form content is valuable, it's important to ensure that it doesn't overwhelm readers. Use clear headings, a table of contents, and anchor links to help users navigate the content easily.

The Importance of Content Updates and Repurposing

Content updates and repurposing are essential for maintaining the relevance and effectiveness of your content over time. Regularly updating your content not only improves its SEO value but also ensures that it continues to meet the needs of your audience.

1. Updating Existing Content:

- **Why It Matters:** Search engines favor fresh, up-to-date content. Regularly updating your content with new information, data, and examples can help you maintain or improve your rankings. According to a 2023 study by Search Engine Journal, updating old blog posts can increase organic traffic by up to 111%.

- **How to Implement:** Review your top-performing content periodically to identify opportunities for updates. This could involve adding new sections, updating outdated information, or improving the overall quality of the content. Use tools like Google Analytics to track the performance of updated content and measure its impact.

2. Repurposing Content Across Platforms:

- **Why It Matters:** Repurposing content allows you to reach different audiences across various platforms while maximizing the value of your original content. For example, a blog post can be repurposed into a video, infographic, or podcast episode, extending its reach and impact.

- **How to Implement:** Identify high-performing content that can be adapted for other formats. For instance, turn a detailed blog post into a series of social media posts, or create a webinar based on a comprehensive guide. Repurposing content not only saves time but also helps reinforce your message across multiple channels.

Case Studies of Successful Content-Driven SEO Strategies

To illustrate the power of integrating content marketing with SEO, let's look at a few real-world examples:

1. HubSpot's Inbound Marketing Blog:

- **Overview:** HubSpot's blog is a prime example of how content marketing and SEO can work together to drive traffic and generate leads. By consistently publishing high-quality, SEO-optimized content on topics

related to inbound marketing, HubSpot has established itself as a thought leader in the industry.
- **Results:** HubSpot's blog attracts millions of visitors each month, many of whom convert into leads and customers. The company's focus on creating valuable, evergreen content has also helped it rank for thousands of competitive keywords.

2. Backlinko's Skyscraper Technique:

- **Overview:** Backlinko, an SEO training company, used the Skyscraper Technique to create a comprehensive guide on Google's ranking factors. By improving upon existing content and promoting it to relevant audiences, Backlinko earned hundreds of high-quality backlinks.
- **Results:** The guide quickly became one of the most linked-to pages in the SEO industry, driving significant organic traffic and establishing Backlinko as a go-to resource for SEO information.

3. Moz's Beginner's Guide to SEO:

- **Overview:** Moz's Beginner's Guide to SEO is an evergreen resource that has been updated and expanded over the years. The guide covers all aspects of SEO in a comprehensive, easy-to-understand format, making it accessible to beginners and experts alike.
- **Results:** The guide ranks highly for numerous SEO-related keywords and has been linked to by thousands of websites, contributing to Moz's authority and visibility in the industry.

Integrating Content Marketing and SEO for Maximum Impact

Integrating content marketing with SEO is essential for creating content that not only ranks well but also resonates with your audience. By aligning your content with user intent, optimizing it for SEO, and regularly updating and repurposing it, you can drive long-term traffic, build authority, and achieve your business goals. In the next chapter, we'll dive into the various SEO tools available and how to use them effectively to enhance your content marketing and SEO efforts.

Chapter 8: SEO Tools and How to Use Them

Having the right tools at your disposal can make all the difference. SEO tools help streamline your workflow, provide valuable insights, and enable you to make data-driven decisions that enhance your website's performance. According to a 2024 report by SEMrush, 73% of businesses that invest in SEO tools see a measurable improvement in their search rankings within six months. This chapter will explore essential SEO tools for various purposes, including keyword research, site audits, backlink analysis, and content optimization, and offer tips on how to use them effectively.

Overview of Essential SEO Tools

SEO tools come in many forms, from free utilities to comprehensive platforms that offer a suite of features. These tools are designed to help you analyze, optimize, and monitor different aspects of your SEO strategy. Below, we'll break down some of the most commonly used SEO tools and how they can benefit your website.

1. Google Analytics and Google Search Console:

- **Google Analytics:**
    - **What It Is:** Google Analytics is a free web analytics tool that tracks and reports website traffic. It provides insights into user behavior, acquisition channels, and conversion rates, making it an essential tool for any SEO strategy.
    - **How to Use:** Use Google Analytics to monitor key metrics like page views, bounce rate, and average session duration. The "Acquisition" report helps you understand where your traffic is coming from (organic search, direct, social, etc.), while the "Behavior" report shows how users interact with your content. Set up goals and conversions to track specific actions, such as form submissions or purchases, and assess the ROI of your SEO efforts.

- **Google Search Console:**
    - **What It Is:** Google Search Console (GSC) is a free tool that helps you monitor, maintain, and troubleshoot your site's presence in Google Search results. It provides insights into how

Google crawls and indexes your site and highlights any issues that may affect your rankings.
- **How to Use:** Use GSC to track keyword rankings, click-through rates (CTR), and impressions. The "Coverage" report identifies indexing issues, such as pages that are blocked by robots.txt or have errors. The "Performance" report shows which queries are driving traffic to your site, allowing you to optimize for high-performing keywords. Regularly check the "Core Web Vitals" report to ensure your site meets Google's performance standards.

2. Ahrefs:

- **Overview:** Ahrefs is a comprehensive SEO toolset known for its powerful backlink analysis and keyword research capabilities. It's widely used by SEO professionals to track rankings, analyze competitors, and identify link-building opportunities.

- **Key Features:**
  - **Site Explorer:** Ahrefs' Site Explorer allows you to analyze any website's backlink profile, including your competitors. It shows the total number of backlinks, referring domains, and the anchor text used in those links. Use this feature to identify high-quality backlinks and replicate your competitors' successful strategies.
  - **Keywords Explorer:** This tool provides keyword ideas, search volume, keyword difficulty, and click-through rates. It's useful for finding profitable keywords that are relevant to your niche and understanding the competitive landscape.
  - **Content Explorer:** Content Explorer helps you find top-performing content in your industry, based on social shares and backlinks. Use this tool to identify trending topics and create content that resonates with your audience.

- **How to Use:** Use Ahrefs to conduct a thorough backlink audit, identify toxic links, and disavow them if necessary. Analyze your competitors' backlink profiles to find link-building opportunities, and use the Keywords Explorer to refine your keyword strategy. Regularly monitor your site's health using Ahrefs' Site Audit feature to identify and fix technical SEO issues.

3. SEMrush:

- **Overview:** SEMrush is an all-in-one marketing platform that offers a wide range of tools for SEO, content marketing, social media management, and more. It's particularly popular for its keyword research, site audit, and competitor analysis features.

- **Key Features:**
    - **Keyword Magic Tool:** SEMrush's Keyword Magic Tool generates keyword ideas based on a seed keyword. It provides data on search volume, keyword difficulty, and SERP features, helping you find the best keywords to target.
    - **Site Audit:** SEMrush's Site Audit tool scans your website for technical issues, such as broken links, duplicate content, and mobile usability problems. It provides a detailed report with recommendations for improving your site's health.
    - **Position Tracking:** This tool allows you to track your keyword rankings over time, monitor your competitors' performance, and receive notifications of any significant changes in your rankings.

- **How to Use:** Use SEMrush's Keyword Magic Tool to build a list of target keywords, and the Site Audit tool to identify and fix technical issues. The Position Tracking feature helps you monitor your progress and make adjustments to your SEO strategy as needed. Additionally, SEMrush's Backlink Analytics tool can be used to find new link-building opportunities and analyze your competitors' backlink strategies.

4. Moz:

- **Overview:** Moz offers a suite of SEO tools that include keyword research, site audits, link building, and rank tracking. Moz is known for its user-friendly interface and helpful resources, such as the Moz Blog and MozBar, a free SEO toolbar.

- **Key Features:**
    - **Keyword Explorer:** Moz's Keyword Explorer provides keyword suggestions, search volume, difficulty scores, and organic CTR data. It also offers a "Priority" score that combines various metrics to help you identify the best keywords to target.
    - **Link Explorer:** This tool allows you to explore your backlink profile, track new and lost links, and analyze your site's domain

authority (DA). Moz's DA metric is widely used in the industry to assess the authority of websites.
    - **On-Page Grader:** Moz's On-Page Grader evaluates individual pages on your site for on-page SEO factors, such as keyword usage, meta tags, and internal links. It provides actionable recommendations for improving your on-page optimization.
- **How to Use:** Use Moz's Keyword Explorer to build a keyword strategy that balances search volume, difficulty, and relevance. The Link Explorer helps you monitor your backlink profile and identify link-building opportunities. The On-Page Grader can be used to fine-tune your content and ensure it's fully optimized for your target keywords.

5. Screaming Frog SEO Spider:

- **Overview:** Screaming Frog SEO Spider is a powerful website crawler that helps you audit your website for technical SEO issues. It's particularly useful for large sites with complex structures, as it can crawl and analyze thousands of pages in a short amount of time.
- **Key Features:**
    - **Crawling:** Screaming Frog crawls your website and provides detailed reports on issues like broken links, duplicate content, missing meta tags, and redirects. It also analyzes the site's internal linking structure and identifies orphaned pages.
    - **XML Sitemap Generation:** The tool can generate XML sitemaps that include all important pages on your site, helping search engines crawl and index your content more efficiently.
    - **Integration:** Screaming Frog integrates with Google Analytics, Google Search Console, and Ahrefs to provide even more insights into your site's performance.
- **How to Use:** Use Screaming Frog to perform a comprehensive site audit, identifying and fixing issues that could impact your SEO. Generate an XML sitemap and submit it to Google Search Console to ensure your site is fully indexed. The tool's integration with other platforms allows you to combine data for a more holistic view of your site's health.

Tips for Selecting the Right SEO Tools

With so many SEO tools available, choosing the right ones for your needs can be overwhelming. Here are some tips to help you select the best tools for your SEO strategy:

1. Assess Your Needs and Goals:

- **What to Consider:** Start by assessing your specific needs and goals. Are you focused on keyword research, backlink building, technical SEO, or content optimization? Understanding your priorities will help you narrow down your options.

- **How to Apply:** If your primary goal is keyword research, tools like Ahrefs, SEMrush, or Moz are excellent choices. For technical SEO, consider Screaming Frog or Google Search Console. If you're on a tight budget, free tools like Google Analytics and MozBar can provide valuable insights without the cost.

2. Compare Features and Pricing:

- **What to Consider:** Compare the features and pricing of different tools to find the best fit for your budget and needs. Some tools offer free versions or trials, allowing you to test them out before committing to a paid plan.

- **How to Apply:** Create a list of must-have features and compare how different tools stack up. Consider whether you need an all-in-one platform like SEMrush or specialized tools like Screaming Frog. Keep in mind that investing in the right tools can save you time and improve your SEO results in the long run.

3. Consider Ease of Use and Support:

- **What to Consider:** The best SEO tool is one that you can use effectively. Consider the tool's user interface, ease of use, and the quality of customer support available. Some tools offer extensive tutorials, guides, and community forums to help you get the most out of them.

- **How to Apply:** If you're new to SEO, look for tools with a user-friendly interface and strong customer support. Moz, for example, is known for its intuitive design and helpful resources, making it a great choice for beginners. More advanced users may prefer tools like Ahrefs or SEMrush, which offer powerful features but may have a steeper learning curve.

Leveraging SEO Tools for Success

SEO tools are indispensable for optimizing your website, analyzing your competitors, and making informed decisions that drive better results. By selecting the right tools for your needs and using them effectively, you can enhance your SEO strategy, improve your search rankings, and achieve your digital marketing goals. In the next chapter, we'll explore how to measure and track SEO success, focusing on key metrics, tools for tracking performance, and strategies for reporting results to stakeholders.

Chapter 9: Measuring and Tracking SEO Success

Measuring and tracking the success of your SEO efforts is crucial for understanding what's working, identifying areas for improvement, and demonstrating the value of your strategy to stakeholders. Without clear metrics and regular analysis, it's impossible to know whether your efforts are driving the desired results. According to a 2023 report by HubSpot, 75% of marketers say they are more likely to achieve their marketing goals when they consistently measure and track their performance. In this chapter, we'll explore the key metrics to track for SEO success, tools for monitoring your performance, and strategies for reporting your results effectively.

Key Metrics to Track for SEO Success

SEO success isn't just about ranking for keywords; it's about achieving meaningful results that align with your business goals. Here are the key metrics you should be tracking to measure the effectiveness of your SEO strategy:

1. Organic Traffic:

- **What It Is:** Organic traffic refers to the number of visitors who come to your website from search engines without any paid promotion. It's a direct indicator of your SEO efforts and is often the primary goal of SEO campaigns.

- **How to Track It:** Use Google Analytics to monitor your organic traffic over time. Look at the "Acquisition" report under the "Organic Search" section to see how many users are visiting your site through organic search. Pay attention to trends and identify any spikes or drops in traffic, which may indicate the impact of algorithm updates or changes in your SEO strategy.

2. Keyword Rankings:

- **What It Is:** Keyword rankings refer to the position your website holds in search engine results pages (SERPs) for specific keywords. Higher rankings generally lead to more visibility and traffic.

- **How to Track It:** Tools like Ahrefs, SEMrush, and Moz allow you to track your keyword rankings over time. Monitor your rankings for high-priority keywords and assess how changes in your content or SEO tactics affect your position in the SERPs. Remember that rankings can fluctuate, so focus on overall trends rather than day-to-day changes.

3. Click-Through Rate (CTR):

- **What It Is:** CTR is the percentage of users who click on your link after seeing it in the search results. A high CTR indicates that your title tags and meta descriptions are compelling and relevant to the user's query.

- **How to Track It:** Google Search Console provides insights into your CTR for individual keywords and pages. Review the "Performance" report to see which queries have the highest and lowest CTR. If your CTR is low, consider optimizing your title tags and meta descriptions to make them more appealing and relevant to the search intent.

4. Bounce Rate:

- **What It Is:** Bounce rate is the percentage of visitors who leave your website after viewing only one page. A high bounce rate can indicate that users aren't finding what they're looking for or that the page isn't meeting their expectations.

- **How to Track It:** Google Analytics tracks bounce rate under the "Behavior" report. Analyze the bounce rate for individual pages to identify content that may need improvement. While a high bounce rate isn't always bad—especially for pages like blog posts where the user gets the information they need quickly—it can signal issues with user experience or content quality.

5. Conversion Rate:

- **What It Is:** Conversion rate refers to the percentage of visitors who complete a desired action on your website, such as making a purchase, filling out a form, or signing up for a newsletter. It's one of the most important metrics for measuring the effectiveness of your SEO strategy.

- **How to Track It:** Set up goals in Google Analytics to track conversions based on specific actions. Monitor your conversion rate to see how well your SEO efforts are driving meaningful interactions with your site. If your conversion rate is low, consider optimizing your landing pages, calls-to-action (CTAs), and overall user experience.

6. Backlinks:

- **What It Is:** Backlinks are links from other websites to your own. They are a key factor in determining your site's authority and rankings in search engines. High-quality backlinks from reputable sites can significantly boost your SEO performance.
- **How to Track It:** Use tools like Ahrefs, Moz, or SEMrush to monitor your backlink profile. Track the number of new and lost backlinks over time and assess the quality of the sites linking to you. A healthy backlink profile should consist of links from a diverse range of authoritative websites.

7. Page Load Time and Core Web Vitals:

- **What It Is:** Page load time refers to how long it takes for your website to load. Core Web Vitals are a set of metrics introduced by Google to measure the user experience, including loading speed, interactivity, and visual stability.
- **How to Track It:** Use Google's PageSpeed Insights and Core Web Vitals reports in Google Search Console to assess your site's performance. Aim for a fast-loading site with low LCP (Largest Contentful Paint), FID (First Input Delay), and CLS (Cumulative Layout Shift) scores. Improving these metrics can enhance user experience and potentially boost your rankings.

Tools for Monitoring SEO Performance

Tracking SEO metrics manually can be time-consuming and challenging. Fortunately, there are several tools available to help you monitor your performance and stay on top of key metrics. Here are some of the most effective tools for tracking SEO success:

1. Google Analytics:

- **Overview:** Google Analytics is an essential tool for monitoring your website's performance. It provides detailed insights into organic traffic, user behavior, conversion rates, and more.
- **How to Use:** Set up custom dashboards to track the metrics that matter most to your SEO strategy. Use segmentation to analyze traffic from different sources, devices, and locations. Regularly review your reports to identify trends and areas for improvement.

2. Google Search Console:

- **Overview:** Google Search Console is a free tool that provides insights into your site's search performance, indexing status, and technical issues. It's invaluable for tracking keyword rankings, CTR, and Core Web Vitals.
- **How to Use:** Regularly check the "Performance" report to monitor your keyword rankings and CTR. Use the "Coverage" report to identify indexing issues, and the "Core Web Vitals" report to track your site's user experience metrics. Set up alerts to be notified of any critical issues that need immediate attention.

3. SEMrush:

- **Overview:** SEMrush is an all-in-one marketing platform that offers a wide range of tools for SEO tracking, including rank tracking, backlink analysis, and site audits.
- **How to Use:** Use SEMrush's Position Tracking tool to monitor your keyword rankings across different devices and locations. The Backlink Analytics tool allows you to track your backlink profile and identify new link-building opportunities. Regularly run site audits to detect and fix technical SEO issues that could impact your performance.

4. Ahrefs:

- **Overview:** Ahrefs is a comprehensive SEO toolset that excels in backlink analysis, keyword tracking, and content research.
- **How to Use:** Use Ahrefs' Site Explorer to monitor your backlink profile and assess the quality of your inbound links. The Keywords Explorer tool helps you track your rankings for target keywords and identify new opportunities. The Content Explorer feature allows you to analyze top-performing content in your niche and find inspiration for new content ideas.

5. Moz:

- **Overview:** Moz offers a suite of SEO tools, including rank tracking, keyword research, and site audits. It's known for its user-friendly interface and helpful resources.
- **How to Use:** Use Moz's Rank Tracker to monitor your keyword rankings over time and compare your performance against competitors. The Link Explorer tool helps you track your backlink profile and identify

high-quality linking opportunities. Use the On-Page Grader to evaluate and optimize individual pages on your site.

Strategies for Reporting SEO Results to Stakeholders

Effective reporting is crucial for communicating the value of your SEO efforts to stakeholders. Whether you're reporting to clients, executives, or team members, it's important to present your data in a clear and actionable way. Here are some strategies for reporting SEO results:

1. Focus on Key Metrics and KPIs:

- **What to Do:** Identify the key performance indicators (KPIs) that are most relevant to your stakeholders and align with your business goals. These might include organic traffic, conversion rates, keyword rankings, or ROI.
- **How to Apply:** Create reports that highlight these KPIs and explain how your SEO efforts are contributing to overall business success. Use visual aids like charts and graphs to make the data more digestible and emphasize trends and outcomes.

2. Provide Context and Insights:

- **What to Do:** Data alone isn't enough—you need to provide context and insights to help stakeholders understand what the numbers mean. Explain the significance of key metrics, any notable trends, and the impact of your SEO activities.
- **How to Apply:** For example, if there's a spike in organic traffic, explain whether it's due to a successful content campaign, a technical SEO fix, or a seasonal trend. If rankings for certain keywords have improved, highlight the specific optimizations that led to those gains.

3. Use Dashboards for Real-Time Reporting:

- **What to Do:** Dashboards provide a real-time overview of your SEO performance and allow stakeholders to track progress without waiting for periodic reports.
- **How to Apply:** Use tools like Google Data Studio, SEMrush, or Ahrefs to create custom dashboards that display key metrics. Share these dashboards with stakeholders so they can monitor performance and stay informed about ongoing SEO activities.

4. Set Clear Goals and Benchmarks:

- **What to Do:** Establish clear goals and benchmarks for your SEO strategy, and use these as reference points in your reports. This helps stakeholders understand whether you're meeting expectations and progressing toward long-term objectives.
- **How to Apply:** At the start of your SEO campaign, set specific, measurable goals (e.g., "Increase organic traffic by 20% in six months" or "Rank in the top three for five target keywords"). Regularly report on your progress toward these goals and adjust your strategy as needed.

5. Tailor Reports to Your Audience:

- **What to Do:** Different stakeholders have different priorities, so it's important to tailor your reports to meet their specific needs and interests.
- **How to Apply:** For executives, focus on high-level metrics like ROI and business impact. For clients, emphasize progress on agreed-upon goals and highlight specific achievements. For team members, provide more detailed insights into day-to-day performance and areas for improvement.

Measuring SEO Success for Continuous Improvement

Measuring and tracking SEO success is essential for understanding the effectiveness of your strategy and making informed decisions that drive continuous improvement. By focusing on key metrics, using the right tools, and reporting results effectively, you can demonstrate the value of your SEO efforts and achieve your business goals. In the final chapter, we'll explore how to stay updated with SEO trends, focusing on the ever-changing nature of SEO and the importance of continuous learning and adaptation.

Chapter 10: Staying Updated with SEO Trends

SEO is an ever-evolving field, influenced by changes in search engine algorithms, core updates, user behavior, and technological advancements. To remain competitive and achieve long-term success, it's crucial to stay informed about the latest trends and adapt your strategies accordingly. According to a 2023 survey by Search Engine Land, 82% of SEO professionals agree that keeping up with industry trends is essential for maintaining a competitive edge. In this chapter, we'll explore the dynamic nature of SEO, how to stay updated with the latest trends, and resources for ongoing education and learning.

The Ever-Changing Nature of SEO

Search engines like Google frequently update their algorithms to improve the quality of search results and better serve user needs. These updates can have a significant impact on website rankings, making it essential for SEO professionals to stay informed and adapt quickly. Some of the key factors driving changes in SEO include:

1. Algorithm Updates:

- **Core Updates:** Google's core algorithm updates can have a widespread impact on search rankings. These updates, which occur several times a year, aim to refine how Google evaluates and ranks content. For example, Google's Helpful Content Update in 2023 prioritized content created for users over content created solely for SEO purposes. It's important to monitor these updates and adjust your strategy as needed to maintain or improve your rankings.

- **Targeted Updates:** In addition to core updates, Google releases targeted updates that focus on specific aspects of SEO, such as page experience, mobile-friendliness, or site speed. For instance, the Page Experience Update in 2021 emphasized the importance of Core Web Vitals, which measure loading performance, interactivity, and visual stability.

2. User Behavior and Search Intent:

- **Evolving Search Behavior:** User behavior and search intent are constantly evolving. For example, the rise of voice search and mobile search has changed the way people interact with search engines. In 2024, it's estimated that 55% of households will have a smart speaker, leading to more voice-based queries. SEO strategies must adapt to these changes by focusing on conversational keywords and optimizing for mobile devices.

- **Personalization:** Search engines are increasingly using personalization to deliver more relevant results based on a user's search history, location, and preferences. This means that search results can vary significantly from one user to another, making it essential to understand your audience and tailor your content to meet their specific needs.

3. Technological Advancements:

- **AI and Machine Learning:** Artificial intelligence (AI) and machine learning are playing an increasingly important role in SEO. Google's AI-driven RankBrain algorithm, for example, helps process and understand complex search queries. To stay competitive, SEO professionals must understand how AI influences search rankings and consider incorporating AI-powered tools into their strategies.

- **Structured Data and Schema Markup:** Structured data and schema markup help search engines understand the content on your website and enhance how it's displayed in search results. By implementing schema markup, you can increase your chances of appearing in rich snippets, knowledge panels, and other enhanced search features.

How to Stay Updated with SEO Trends

Keeping up with the latest SEO trends requires a proactive approach. Here are some strategies to help you stay informed and ahead of the curve:

1. Follow Industry Blogs and Publications:

- **What to Do:** Industry blogs and publications are among the best sources for the latest SEO news, insights, and best practices. Leading publications often provide detailed analyses of algorithm updates, case studies, and expert opinions on emerging trends.

- **Recommended Resources:**
    - **Search Engine Land:** A leading publication that covers the latest news in search marketing, including algorithm updates, SEO strategies, and industry trends.
    - **Moz Blog:** Moz offers valuable insights into SEO, content marketing, and digital marketing strategies, with a focus on actionable advice and real-world examples.

- **Search Engine Journal:** Provides in-depth articles, how-tos, and news related to search engines, SEO, and digital marketing.
- **Ahrefs Blog:** Known for its data-driven articles and case studies, Ahrefs Blog is a go-to resource for advanced SEO techniques and strategies.

2. Participate in Webinars and Online Courses:

- **What to Do:** Webinars and online courses are excellent opportunities to learn from industry experts and stay updated on the latest SEO techniques. Many SEO tool providers and digital marketing agencies offer free or paid webinars on topics ranging from keyword research to technical SEO.

- **Recommended Platforms:**
  - **HubSpot Academy:** Offers free online courses on SEO, content marketing, and inbound marketing. These courses are designed for beginners and experienced marketers alike.
  - **SEMrush Academy:** Provides free courses and certification programs on SEO, content marketing, PPC, and more. These courses are led by industry experts and include practical tips and best practices.
  - **Yoast SEO Academy:** Focuses on SEO training with a range of free and premium courses covering topics like technical SEO, keyword research, and SEO copywriting.

3. Engage with SEO Communities and Forums:

- **What to Do:** Engaging with SEO communities and forums allows you to connect with other professionals, share knowledge, and stay updated on the latest industry developments. These communities often discuss recent algorithm changes, share case studies, and provide support for SEO challenges.

- **Recommended Communities:**
  - **SEO Reddit:** The SEO subreddit is a popular forum where professionals discuss SEO news, share insights, and ask questions. It's a great place to learn from others and stay informed about the latest trends.

- **Moz Community:** Moz's online community offers a platform for SEO professionals to connect, share knowledge, and seek advice on SEO-related topics.
- **SEO Chat Forums:** An active community where SEO professionals discuss a wide range of topics, from technical SEO to content marketing and link building.

4. Attend Industry Conferences and Events:

- **What to Do:** Attending industry conferences and events is an excellent way to stay updated with the latest SEO trends, network with peers, and learn from thought leaders. Many conferences offer workshops, panel discussions, and keynote speeches on cutting-edge SEO strategies.

- **Recommended Events:**
    - **SMX (Search Marketing Expo):** A leading conference series that covers all aspects of search marketing, including SEO, PPC, and content marketing. SMX events are held throughout the year in various locations and online.
    - **MozCon:** Moz's annual conference brings together industry experts to discuss the latest trends in SEO, content marketing, and digital marketing. The event features actionable presentations and networking opportunities.
    - **BrightonSEO:** A popular search marketing conference in the UK, BrightonSEO offers talks and workshops on a wide range of SEO topics, from technical SEO to link building and content strategy.

5. Monitor Algorithm Updates and Industry Changes:

- **What to Do:** Monitoring algorithm updates and industry changes is essential for staying ahead of the curve. Set up alerts and notifications to ensure you're informed as soon as new developments occur.

- **How to Apply:**
    - **Google Alerts:** Set up Google Alerts for terms like "Google algorithm update," "SEO trends," and "search engine news" to receive notifications when new content is published on these topics.

- **Follow Google Search Central Blog:** Google's official blog for webmasters and SEOs provides announcements and updates on algorithm changes, best practices, and new features.
- **Use Tools Like MozCast or SEMrush Sensor:** These tools track fluctuations in search rankings and can help you detect potential algorithm updates before they're officially announced.

The Importance of Continuous Learning and Adaptation

SEO is not a set-it-and-forget-it strategy. To succeed in the long term, you must continuously learn, adapt, and refine your approach based on the latest trends and developments. Here's why continuous learning and adaptation are crucial:

1. Staying Competitive:

- **Why It Matters:** The SEO landscape is highly competitive, with new websites and content being published every day. Staying updated with the latest trends and techniques ensures that you remain competitive and can outperform rivals in the SERPs.
- **How to Apply:** Regularly review your SEO strategy and make adjustments based on new insights, tools, and best practices. Experiment with new tactics and technologies to stay ahead of the competition.

2. Responding to Algorithm Changes:

- **Why It Matters:** Algorithm updates can have a significant impact on your rankings, traffic, and overall SEO performance. Being prepared to respond quickly to these changes can help you mitigate potential losses and capitalize on new opportunities.
- **How to Apply:** Develop a process for monitoring algorithm updates and assessing their impact on your site. When updates occur, analyze how they affect your rankings and make necessary adjustments to your content, technical SEO, or link-building strategy.

3. Embracing New Technologies and Trends:

- **Why It Matters:** Emerging technologies and trends, such as AI, voice search, and mobile-first indexing, are shaping the future of SEO. Embracing these innovations can help you stay relevant and reach new audiences.
- **How to Apply:** Stay informed about technological advancements and consider how they can be integrated into your SEO strategy. For

example, optimize your content for voice search by focusing on conversational keywords, or implement structured data to enhance your visibility in rich snippets.

The Future of SEO and Continuous Growth

The future of SEO is dynamic and full of opportunities. By staying updated with the latest trends, continuously learning, and adapting your strategies, you can position your website for long-term success in the ever-changing digital landscape. As we conclude this book, remember that SEO is a journey, not a destination. Keep experimenting, learning, and refining your approach to achieve sustainable growth and stay ahead in the competitive world of search engine optimization.

Conclusion and Final Thoughts

As we conclude this comprehensive guide to SEO, it's clear that search engine optimization is a multifaceted discipline that requires a strategic, data-driven approach. From understanding the basics to mastering advanced techniques, each chapter of this book has provided insights, tools, and best practices to help you succeed in the world of SEO.

Whether you're just starting your SEO journey or looking to refine your existing strategy, remember that the key to success lies in continuous learning, adaptation, and a commitment to delivering value to your audience. By integrating the principles and strategies outlined in this book into your SEO efforts, you can improve your website's visibility, drive meaningful traffic, and achieve your business goals.

Appendix: Resources and Tools

- **SEO Tools:**
    - Google Analytics: https://analytics.google.com/
    - Google Search Console: https://search.google.com/search-console/
    - Ahrefs: https://ahrefs.com/
    - SEMrush: https://www.semrush.com/
    - Moz: https://moz.com/
    - Screaming Frog SEO Spider: https://www.screamingfrog.co.uk/seo-spider/

- **Further Reading:**
    - Search Engine Land: https://searchengineland.com/
    - Moz Blog: https://moz.com/blog
    - Search Engine Journal: https://www.searchenginejournal.com/
    - Ahrefs Blog: https://ahrefs.com/blog/

- **Citations and References:**
    - **Chapter 1:** Internet Live Stats. (2024). "Google Search Statistics."
    - **Chapter 2:** Ahrefs. (2023). "Why 90.63% of Content Gets No Traffic from Google."
    - **Chapter 3:** Backlinko. (2023). "On-Page SEO: Anatomy of a Perfectly Optimized Page."
    - **Chapter 4:** Google. (2023). "Page Speed Insights and Core Web Vitals."
    - **Chapter 5:** Moz. (2023). "The Importance of Backlinks in SEO."
    - **Chapter 6:** BrightLocal. (2023). "Local Consumer Review Survey."

- **Chapter 7:** HubSpot. (2023). "The Impact of Blogging on ROI."
- **Chapter 8:** SEMrush. (2024). "The Role of SEO Tools in Achieving High Rankings."
- **Chapter 9:** HubSpot. (2023). "The Importance of Measuring Marketing Performance."
- **Chapter 10:** Search Engine Land. (2023). "The Importance of Keeping Up with SEO Trends."

www.ingramcontent.com/pod-product-compliance
Lightning Source LLC
Chambersburg PA
CBHW030051230526
45471CB00003B/1049